So Rare a Treasure

Text and Paintings by

SANDY LYNAM CLOUGH

HARVEST HOUSE PUBLISHERS
Eugene, Oregon

So Rare a Treasure

Copyright © 2000 by Sandy Lynam Clough
Published by Harvest House Publishers
Eugene, Oregon 97402

Library of Congress Cataloging-in-Publication Data

Clough, Sandy Lynam, 1948-
    So rare a treasure / Sandy Lynam Clough.
        p.   cm.
    ISBN 0-7369-0214-7
    1. God—Mercy Meditations.   2. God—Love Meditations.   I. Title.
BT153.M4C57   2000
242—dc21

Design and production by Garborg Design Works, Minneapolis, Minnesota

Unless indicated otherwise, Scripture quotations are from the New American
Standard Bible, © 1960, 1962, 1963, 1968, 1971, 1972, 1973, 1975, 1977
by The Lockman Foundation. Used by permission. Verses marked TLB are
from The Living Bible, Copyright © 1971 owned by assignment by Illinois
Regional Bank N.A. (as trustee). Used by permission of Tyndale House
Publishers, Inc., Wheaton, Illinois 60189. All rights reserved. Verses marked
AMP are from The Amplified Bible. Old Testament copyright © 1965, 1987
by The Zondervan Corporation. The Amplified New Testament copyright ©
1958, 1987 by the Lockman Foundation. Used by permission.

This book is dedicated to Gerrie White

with a grateful heart for all the

treasure she has prayed into my life.

*Make the Almighty your gold
and the Lord your precious silver treasure.*
JOB 22:25 AMP

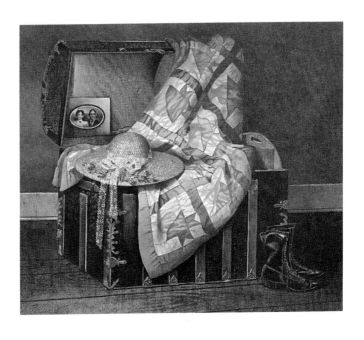

$\mathcal{I}$ want my heart to be an open house,

Filled with treasures rare and pure.

Each room adorned with wonderful truths

And always open for a tour!

Contents

Treasures of the Heart   6

The Little Brown Egg Basket   10

Cabbage Rose Teapot   14

Grandmother's Gold Watch   17

A Clean Platter   20

My Friendship Hankie   24

The Cracked Cup   28

A Necklace Fit for a Queen   33

Mama's Teapot   37

The Silver Cake Basket   39

A New Arrangement   42

The Most Expensive Flowerpot   47

Cups of Affection   50

Beyond Compare   54

A Priceless Treasure   58

The Beautiful Heart   60

The Missing Treasure   62

Treasures of the Heart

There I was in an antique store in Toronto, nearly overwhelmed by the selection of antique china. I had never seen so much dinnerware under one roof! Beautiful platters, ten or twelve deep, stood on edge on the floor against shelves filled with china. Hundreds of teacups and teapots so exquisite (and expensive) were displayed behind glass under lock and key. Everything there seemed to have a pedigree. And yet it didn't even matter whether I could afford them or not—I couldn't find anything I wanted to buy. After asking for German teacups and being shown the Dresdens, I finally gave up and stepped out into the fresh air.

But wait—there outside on the sidewalk were "bargain" teacups, some still wrapped in newspaper and crammed into boxes. I was giving them a half-hearted look when I saw it—a sweet, scalloped little cup and saucer with little pink roses and delicate gold scrollwork. No doubt it was Victorian, and I wasn't surprised to see "Germany" stamped on the cup's bottom. I didn't care that afternoons of tea had worn the gold off! I had finally found something I wanted to buy. This well-used little teacup—a new treasure—was going home to Georgia with me.

Perhaps you're like me, and the most exciting leisure activity you can think of is antiquing. There's a certain charm in visiting old things that were used in more genteel days. To me, a day spent prowling dusty antique stores is well spent, even if I don't buy anything. But there is a smug feeling of victory and joy in the air when I take home a lace doilie or a teacup that touched my heart. It becomes one of my treasures, and I don't waste a moment of sympathy on those who missed it.

I'm not sure when I decided that I wanted to surround myself with the warmth of well-loved things—but it wasn't soon enough! It wasn't soon enough to keep me from spending the first furniture money we had as newlyweds on a used, black vinyl living room set with a mediter-ranean flair, accented by two cheap tables and an ugly orange lamp. It didn't take long to regret that purchase! How I wished I had chosen just one real treasure for my home instead of filling a room with such junk. Ugly is easy to come by and hard to get rid of. But get rid of it I finally did!

Today if you were to come into my home, you would be able to share many of the "treasures" I've picked up since those early days. If you were interested only in antiques, I would show you the solid oak filing cabinet I paid two dollars for, or the old high-top shoes I found in their original box in an old general store. But as much as I love these treasures, I would want to show you more than "things" (even old things). I would want to show you treasures that remind me of my real treasures. In the pages to come, that's just what I'll do. I'll paint some of my favorite collectibles for you, ones that represent something deeper—treasures of the heart.

You see, even though I grew up going to church and being an active church member, I went through a time before I realized the Lord had a design and plan just for me. I allowed a lot of junk to accumulate in the treasure room of my heart—ugly stuff—like unforgiveness, fear, and rejection that kept me from being content and joyful. But when I realized I was missing the wonderful life God had for me by trying to be the author and ruler of my own life, I didn't want to live that way anymore! I gave my life to Him. Out went the junk! He began to furnish my heart with treasures—real treasures of truths revealed to me one at a time that taught me how to live. Each of the lovely old things I want to show you in this book is a window into my heart—where the real treasures wait to be shared.

The Little Brown Egg Basket

Every spring I used to travel from wherever I was living at the time to exhibit my paintings at the Vicksburg Flea Market in historic Vicksburg, Mississippi, not far from my hometown. My father would bring his paintings, too; my mother would pack cold drinks, sandwiches, and cookies; and our family would enjoy a day together that began before daylight and ended when we were tired, dusty, and happy. We were usually happy because whether we had sold many paintings or not, we had found some antique treasures.

The annual Vicksburg Flea Market welcomes not only artists and craftsmen, but also antique dealers. In fact, every year before the show actually began we all wanted to be the first to see what antique "finds" were being

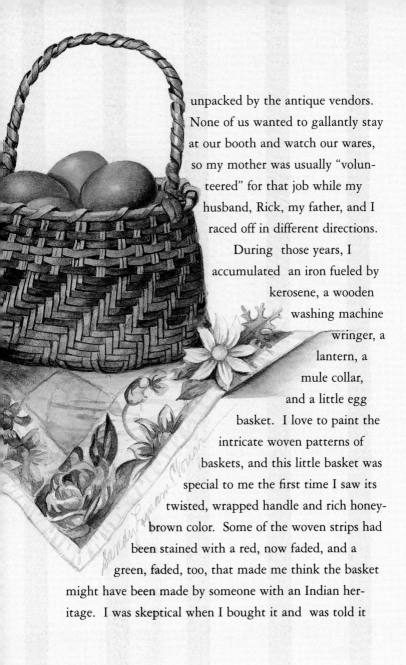

unpacked by the antique vendors. None of us wanted to gallantly stay at our booth and watch our wares, so my mother was usually "volunteered" for that job while my husband, Rick, my father, and I raced off in different directions. During those years, I accumulated an iron fueled by kerosene, a wooden washing machine wringer, a lantern, a mule collar, and a little egg basket. I love to paint the intricate woven patterns of baskets, and this little basket was special to me the first time I saw its twisted, wrapped handle and rich honey-brown color. Some of the woven strips had been stained with a red, now faded, and a green, faded, too, that made me think the basket might have been made by someone with an Indian heritage. I was skeptical when I bought it and was told it was an egg basket. It seemed too small to hold many eggs from a morning trip to the henhouse. But when I took it home and tried putting eggs in it, it held a dozen! I was amazed at what that little brown basket could hold! I don't keep chickens, but that little basket has served me well. Every time I put it in one of my paintings, the painting sells!

Recently I endured some very difficult times when I wondered if my painting would come to an end. After three surgeries to save the vision in one of my eyes, I ended up with damaged vision in that eye and very real fears for the other one. As I struggled with questions about my future, I asked the Lord to make me a yielded vessel; not a silver vessel, not a golden vessel, but a yielded vessel. God led me to His words in the book of

Psalms. There I found peace, rest, and hope for my future. He also reminded me of His love for me in the sacrifice of His Son and assured me of His watchful care in my present circumstances. Although my time in the land of affliction is not over, I can say with gratitude that the Lord has ended my storm of fear and stress, and the sun is shining.

At a recent ladies' retreat, I shared my story with the title "Lord, How Can I Trust You When Everything Keeps Getting Worse!" in a room with standing room only. Afterward women came to me and shared their own stories of pain. One had lost the only baby she could ever have; one had almost died; one had experienced the murder of her four-year-old child. As I asked myself, "How much pain is there under this roof?" I was humbled to realize that my own suffering was small compared to the suffering of many other people. God had not let me suffer until I was absolutely destroyed, as I had feared. He had permitted me to suffer just enough to fill a yielded vessel with hope and confidence in His very character. Now I can offer that hope to others who hurt. Just like my little brown basket, I can offer Him good service and I never cease to be amazed at all the hope and encouragement a plain, yielded vessel can hold.

Cabbage Rose Teapot

If you've ever hunted for old Victorian teapots, you know that every one you see is a treasure! Every one I have is special to me, and I can tell you right where I found it. But only one is my favorite, and it is the first one I ever bought. It is a charming little German teapot with a scalloped top and beautiful cabbage roses on the front. Its colors are soft, and it's just big enough to serve two at a cozy tea.

I never tire of painting this little teapot. It appears over and over in my work because to me it's everything a teapot ought to be. I move it from place to place in my home to show it off to its best advantage in different lights and settings. It simply delights me every time I look at it. But just the other day it occurred to me that although I have poured tea from some of my other old teapots, I have never made tea in this little pot. I have loved it, treasured it, admired it, displayed it, and painted it in paintings, but I have never let it be what it really is—a teapot!

Shortly after we moved into the Victorian-style home my husband so diligently built for us, we invited friends to visit us while they were in town for a week of business and ministry. We were so excited to finally have enough space to share and to provide a home base for them. I even planned meals in advance and enjoyed stocking the cupboards for this visit. My husband and I both work at home with our family art business. We knew having house guests would have an impact on our work schedule, but we really wanted to serve our friends and to enjoy their fellowship and company.

As each day passed, we hoped that they would carve out some time for fellowship with us, but their schedule got busier and busier. My husband looked for a opportunity to offer his help in an upcoming situation they were facing but finally gave up. The week went by, and it was time for them to go. We invited them to stay longer, but they couldn't. As we waved goodbye on Saturday, we ended our week with disappointment. Though we still loved them, we were sad that they had not had time for us to really enjoy their company.

The disappointment lingered for a while, but it wasn't long before the Lord let me see myself. It wasn't a

self-sacrificing hostess that I saw. What I saw was that I treated my Lord, the King of kings, the way my guests had treated me. I rushed in and out of His presence, interrupting my visits with Him whenever something that seemed more important called. Although I loved Him and talked about Him and wanted Him to guide my life, I wasn't letting Him be everything He is and that He wants to be to me— just as I had never let my teapot be a teapot.

Grandmother's Gold Watch

The most special antique in my possession is not even mine. And in this case, believe me, possession is not nine-tenths of the law! I have my grandmother's gold watch. It is a beautiful timepiece with exquisite engravings on the cover. It looks like a man's pocket watch, only it's smaller and more delicate.

My grandmother's name was Ada, and I can see the watch pinned to her high-necked Victorian dress in a portrait of her and my grandfather before my father was born. I remember

my own mother wearing the watch on a heavy gold chain around her neck when I was growing up. But I don't dare wear it for fear of losing it or damaging it, and I would certainly never lend it to anyone. Although I have it, it belongs to my father. He lets me keep it so I can paint it in my paintings. In fact, I can't even assume that one day it will be passed down to me because I'm not an only child. But for now, this piece of our family history is mine—not to own, not to share, but to hold.

Several years ago I enjoyed a leisurely day of shopping and lunch with my best friend. As the day passed, we talked on and on. Proverbs 10:19 says, "When there are many words, transgression is unavoidable, but he who restrains his lips is wise." How I wish I had remembered that and quit while I was ahead! Before that cozy little chat was over, I had shared a confidence about my husband's family history that he had chosen not to share with people. It wasn't anything immoral or illegal; it was just something the family felt best to keep private. After I got home, I got a sinking feeling about what I had done. How could I have done that?

As I waited for my husband to come home so I could confess my error and ask for forgiveness, I figured out why that information had slipped out. Up until that time, a secret was not something I didn't tell—it was something I told only to my best friends. My husband forgave me, but more than that, I learned what a confidence really is. A confidence is something that is given to us, not to own, not to share, but to hold. Just like my grandmother's watch.

A Clean Platter

I once found a large oval platter in
Alabama that is beautifully decorated with
soft pink roses, lily of the valley, and gold
trim. Not only is it old, it has been well
used. The glaze is crackled and the platter dis-
colored from being set too close to the
stove. I like to think of the platter piled
high with fried chicken and biscuits for a
big Sunday dinner. I can imagine a mother
offering her family this wonderful comfort
food that she had probably started very early
that morning, even before church. It reminded me that we
only put on platters what we are willing to offer to others
without expecting anything in return—except an empty
platter, ready to be filled with more wonderful things.

Several years ago our family was really excited to have
finally saved enough money for a new car—not a brand
new car, but a new-to-us car. The model we were driving

had seen its seventeenth birthday. I knew what I wanted. I wanted a Cadillac, a big one. At that time our best friends from Florida were in the wholesale car business. When they realized we were ready to purchase a car, they offered to find us just what we wanted. And find it they did. Or at least we thought they did.

We went to the bank and transferred the eight thousand dollars in cash. (If you're wondering how anybody could buy a car with eight thousand dollars, remember I said it was several years ago!) It looked as though we might have our car before Christmas. But something seemed to be wrong. There were delays in the transaction, and, although we had asked for our money back, by the new year we didn't have a car or eight thousand dollars. We had been betrayed by our friends. Apparently they had taken our money and purchased other cars for their business. All of our appeals to them went unheeded. Our hearts were wounded deeply by this action on the part of people for whom we cared so deeply.

After a few weeks, possibly motivated by a fear of prosecution, Joe returned all but five hundred dollars. Although we were thrilled to have the bulk of the money back, five hundred dollars was still five hundred dollars. It was not likely that we would ever see that money again. Finally I offered the five-hundred-dollar debt to the Lord. I promised Him that if we ever got the money back, I would give it to Him. As far as I was concerned, we were no longer owed any money. I had offered up the debt to the Lord, and He gave me back an empty platter, a clean platter that was able to hold forgiveness for my friends.

A year or two later, I was surprised to receive a letter from them. We had not heard anything from them since the incident. The wife explained that she still had some of my art prints in her possession and that they had been damaged in storage. She said that if I would send her the prices of each one, the insurance company would pay for them and she would send me a check. When I figured up the total of the prints, it was close to five hundred dollars! I planned to be true to my word and give the money to the Lord once I received the payment.

Well, if the insurance company gave my friend any money for my prints, she kept it! Once again I had to offer the debt to the Lord so He could give me back a clean platter ready to offer more forgiveness. One day I surprised myself when out of the blue I said to the Lord, "Please bless these friends!" My platter indeed now held a full serving of forgiveness.

Experience has taught me that there are two kinds of people who pile hurts on others and never ask for forgiveness. One is the kind that doesn't care, and the other is the kind that is unaware that they have caused any pain. Neither will remove their debts by apologizing or trying to make things right.

Sometimes it seems as though my platter is so heavy with hurts that it's all I can do to hold it up long enough to say, "Lord, please take these debts away! They are too heavy for me to carry." But when I do that, expecting no payment or justice in return, my platter is returned to me clean. Then I can fill it with what I want to offer to my friends and family—love and forgiveness.

If you are weary with the weight of hurts, let the Lord help you lift your platter up so He can wipe the debts away and make you free from both careless and unintentional hurts.

Not only can you be free from pain, you can also be free to offer love even to those who have hurt you.

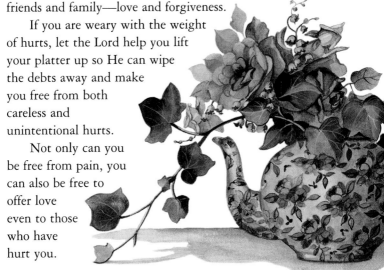

My Friendship Hankie

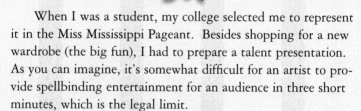

When I was a student, my college selected me to represent it in the Miss Mississippi Pageant. Besides shopping for a new wardrobe (the big fun), I had to prepare a talent presentation. As you can imagine, it's somewhat difficult for an artist to provide spellbinding entertainment for an audience in three short minutes, which is the legal limit.

After considerable brainstorming in the art department, we came up with the idea of a monologue about the song "The Impossible Dream" from the musical *Man from La Mancha*. I would deliver this monologue in front of a twelve-foot long painting that I would paint in advance. At the end of the speech, in a dramatic, innovative move, I would "reach for the unreachable star." At that moment, my hand would pull from my pocket a fistful of glitter to be flung onto a wet-glue spot

Sandy Lynam Clough

on the painting. *Voilá! A star!*

During the preliminary competition at the pageant, everything went perfectly until I cast the glitter in an upward motion toward the sticky spot—and missed! The glitter fluttered down to the stage, almost like a falling star, and I was reaching for nothing. But I had another chance. Saturday night was the finals—and I missed again!

The next year, I picked myself up, dusted myself off, and decided to try another pageant. Right before the big event, I received a huge home-made greeting card from my art professor and his family. On the cover was "Fear Not" and inside was a photograph of an old lady sitting on a rocking chair on her front porch with a shotgun across her lap. With a stern look on her face, she was a picture of ferocious, toothless fragility. This comical photo was attached to a lovely old lace hankie (obviously a family piece) with these words: "Aunt Em is watching over you with a shotgun full of glitter!"

How grateful I am to have had friends like that—friends who would gently laugh with me at myself and yet encourage me to try, try again. That handkerchief became to me a symbol of their loyal friendship that still remains. Although I'm sure it was once pristine white, it is now a lovely candlelight ivory. It's not a linen handkerchief edged in lace, but a hankie made of strips of different patterns of lace stitched together in rows around a crocheted flower in the middle.

Just as this hankie is made of strips of handmade lace pieced together much like an heirloom quilt, my life has been enhanced by special people, the perfect friend for each place and each season, that God has brought into my life. Each friendship through the years has been unique and woven in just the way I needed, much like the distinct strips of handmade lace in my handkerchief. Attached with stitches of love, each has been added one at a time to the quilt God is making with my life. Even when distance or circumstance has taken a friend from my daily life, I find the beauty of that life and the joy that was added to mine remains with the whole piece, making it more beautiful than it would have been without that person.

My antique handkerchief is the perfect size just as it is. But I know my "friendship hankie" will never stop growing as I embrace precious new friends in each new season of life.

The Cracked Cup

I am not part of ancient history, but wearing hats and gloves was very much a part of my southern upbringing. When I graduated from high school, the whirl of parties for the graduates included many teas for the young ladies. One springtime Saturday afternoon I went to one without the reassurance of having a friend with me. As I entered a room lined with dressed-up young ladies politely perched on the edge of their chairs, I knew I was among acquaintances, but I wasn't sure I was among friends!

No one offered more than just polite conversation, and after the tea was served, I sat quietly holding my teacup and saucer until they began to rattle. I was so embarrassed by my own nervousness that the rattle might as well have been an earthquake! I had wanted so much to be perfect and to be accepted by at least some of the girls, but I was relieved just to leave that party without spilling tea or breaking a beautiful cup! Trying to be perfect is a terrible strain!

I smile when I remember that day because I'm still not able to be perfect. But now I'm not only comfortable with teacups, I collect them! I have even been called the "teacup lady" because I have enjoyed painting so many in my paintings. I really don't know how many teacups I

have, but the one that is the dearest to my heart really started my whole love affair with teacups.

One day when I was the mother of two very little boys, I envisioned the perfect teacup that I would like to paint. I imagined a delicate cup with soft, petite flowers: an elegant cup with a chip and a perfect crack. I wanted to paint a beautiful, fragile cup that was damaged but not broken. Imperfect, but usable. I had seen cups like that all my life, but where was I going to find one when I needed it? I didn't know how to find the perfect cup and then perfectly crack it.

I stopped in at a local antique store one day and asked if they had such a cup. The owner acknowledged that they did! He remembered a little Haviland cup with a crack in it, but he didn't know what his wife had done with it. I went back another day, but he still didn't know where the cup was. I gave up and didn't go back.

One day my husband, Rick, came in with a Burger King bag and said, "Here's your cup!" I had no idea what he was talking about and threw the bag into the trash. When he realized what I had done, he said, "No! That was your cup." I retrieved the bag from the garbage and pulled out the perfect teacup—fragile, with delicate pink roses with a tiny chip and a perfect crack. It has appeared over and over and over in my paintings, and the most fabulous cup in the world could not topple it from its place in my heart.

Yes, I thought chips and cracks were charming (at least to paint!) until the day I suddenly had to have a serious surgery to save the vision in one of my eyes. Now I felt *I* was damaged, just like my little teacup. I was filled with fear, not only wondering how I would function with that kind of damage, but also how other people would react when they learned about it. I was afraid they would lose confidence in me and my work and abandon me because I had a flaw.

The cry of my heart was not "Use me, Lord," it was "Fix me, Lord." In fact, when a friend tried to encourage me by saying how much God teaches us in suffering, I was not that interested. Inside I felt like saying, "Excuse me, but I'm trying to get healed here! Could you please take your lessons about suffering somewhere else?" All I wanted was to be normal again and to be the way I had been before. But I haven't been fixed. Over time the Lord has taught me how to have confidence in Him for my life by letting me see His character. And part of my testimony is now—you guessed it—how much God teaches us and how much He can enrich our lives when we suffer.

When I began to share my personal pain and the way I had found peace and joy,

nobody rejected me because I wasn't perfect. Instead, people felt free to approach me and share their own pain. They now stop me and tell me their stories because they know that my life isn't perfect, either. They tell me that they're "cracked," too, though in different ways. I'm learning that a cracked cup can be a pretty useful cup. The truth is, most of us have a crack or a chip somewhere. If you don't have one now, just wait—you will. But I have very good news! Everyone is comfortable with a cracked cup.

The Lord gave me a verse in the midst of my ordeal that said I would be "fruitful in the land of affliction." It has been true for me. I have had more opportunities to share His love, more business opportunities for my art, and more trust in Him than I have ever had before. I believe that someday Jesus will fix my vision, but right now He's making me fruitful, just as I am.

It occurred to me not long ago that what I have right now is not what I asked for. I asked to be healed. But is all that He has done for me better than what I asked for? I'm beginning to see that it is. If you're suffering from an old chip or a fresh crack, let me encourage you to consider that, just maybe, He has something better for you, too—something that is even better than being fixed.

A Necklace Fit for a Queen

Old jewelry has such a romance to it. It's hard to look at it without wondering if it was a special gift from a suitor or a husband. Was it worn to a ball or a wedding? Did one person hold it always or was it passed down from mother to daughter or granddaughter?

My mother has given me a lovely old necklace that was hers. It looks as if someone placed clear- or red-faceted stones on a series of tiny silver doilies and hung them all on a chain. As a child, I always thought that it looked like something a queen might wear to a ball. The romantic youth of a parent

has a somewhat foggy quality to a child. We all know our parents had a youth, but it just doesn't seem real to us. For some reason, I have never asked my mother to tell me about this necklace. How old is it? Where did she get it? What is it made of? Where did she wear it? Because I've never asked my mother to tell me what she knows, I don't know how to think about this heirloom, and I don't know what to tell my children about it.

One of the most wonderful things I have discovered about being a Christian is that God has a different way of thinking about things than I do, and His way is right and good and true. And I have learned that how I think about something is more important than you might think!

There was a time in my life that was as good as any to feel a little sorry for myself. We had had some difficult economic years because of my husband's job situation. He was having to transition from the profession he

felt God had chosen for him (and that he had trained for) to just making a living. The death of hope of working in that profession was long and painful. Discouragement was sometimes so thick and deep that simple tasks like delivering gifts, keeping up with friends and family, and even mailing bills were huge efforts. When hope had finally passed away, Rick began anew. Working in a new field required us to move. He had to go ahead of us while our two little ones (ages two and four) and I stayed behind several weeks until our house in Georgia became available.

One Sunday while I was balancing being mother and father, artist and moving company, a friend stopped me at church and spoke to me. He mentioned that some people who were close to us were concerned because we had neglected their birthdays and other special occasions. I went home with my two boys and plopped myself down on my bed with grumbling and a rumble of resentment in my heart. "Here I

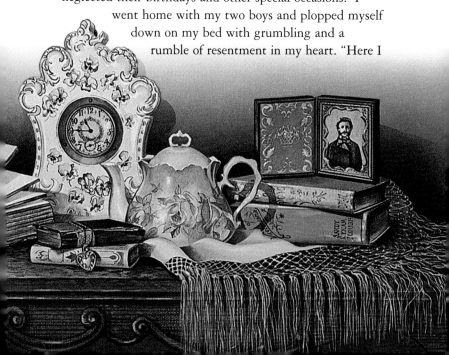

am trying to hold everything together by myself, and they're concerned about their birthdays! They have no idea what we have been through!"

As my personal outburst subsided, my thoughts turned to the devotional book I had been reading. It called to my attention the fact that our thoughts and thinking are not naturally the same as God's. But, as Christians, we can ask God for His wisdom. We can renew our minds. I stopped right there and said, "Lord, I don't know how to think about this situation. Please show me how to think about it."

The upheaval in my mind vanished as I realized these special people were not concerned about gifts or themselves. Their concern was for their relationship with us. What a contrast! My thinking could have damaged the relationships. God's thinking revealed the truth of the matter and made me want to respond to their concern with love.

Isaiah 55:8 tells us: "My thoughts are not your thoughts, neither are your ways My ways...My ways [are] higher than your ways and My thoughts than your thoughts" (AMP).

It is such a privilege to be able to go to God and ask for the truth and the right way to think about something. Try it—it works!

Mama's Teapot

My mother had a pottery teapot shaped like a big fat ear of corn that she kept in a kitchen cabinet. Inside was tucked her "mad" money. We all knew it was there because she wanted us to be able to find money for things like the paperboy collecting for the month. That teapot is mine now, safely stored on a bookshelf in an antique secretary in my parlor. But don't bother checking—it has no money in it!

There was a time when I felt I had to keep the real me as hidden as Mama's money was in that teapot. When I would hear a Christian woman sharing her heart and her testimony, I would think, "Wow! How transparent her life is! She has nothing to hide." Would I ever get to that point? Would I ever have enough confidence to share my heart and not wonder about what people would think if they saw my struggles and what God was teaching me (and needing to teach me).

The Scriptures say in Jeremiah 17:9 that "the heart is the most deceitful thing there is, and desperately wicked" (TLB). I don't think of myself that way. But God's Word makes it clear that my heart is fully capable of breaking all of His commandments. Seeing that has freed me to be honest about myself! No one will ever think as badly of me as I know is possible. What an admonition to walk carefully and with humility.

Do I now think that we all need to recite a litany of the dirty laundry of our lives publicly in order to prove our humility? No, it's not the abandoning of discretion that makes us transparent; it's the absence of pride— the kind of pride that would keep me from sharing the places where I've missed the mark when sharing would help a friend. A teapot is really not made for hiding things anyway—or it would lock! It's designed to pour out refreshment and comfort to those who need it. I want to do that, too. Don't you?

The Silver Cake Basket

For two dollars I came away from a garage sale with a lovely antique silver Victorian cake basket. You may have seen it, filled with roses, in my painting on the cover of the book *If Teacups Could Talk* by Emilie Barnes. It has a beaded silver handle and a footed base and was once used to serve dainty cakes and cookies. I can still use it to serve cake or breads or just admire it filled with fruit or silk flowers. But I can't float flowers in water in it because it was designed with a pierced bottom. It was never meant to hold anything that flows.

This graceful cake basket helps me remember that I am not meant to hold anything that God wants to flow, either. In the earlier years of our marriage, my husband and I experienced unemployment and our first pregnancy at the same time. Rick had been hired as a youth minister by a church in California, but we could not move until after the baby was born. We were determined to be faithful in our own giving and to trust God to provide for our needs in this temporary situation. But one day, late in my pregnancy, I came home and opened the mail. As I read the utility bill and calculated the money we had, I could clearly see the bottom of the barrel. And it was not a pretty sight! I was discouraged and afraid. Rick had been fasting and praying, and as I finished my lunch a Scripture came to my mind: "Stand still, and see the deliverance of the Lord Who is with you" (2 Chronicles 20:17 AMP). Just then a knock came at the front door. Not really wanting company, I stalled and then relented and went to open it. A precious friend greeted me there. As we sat down together on the sofa, she handed me an envelope and said, "This is for you to buy everything you need to go to the hospital. Give what is left to Rick to pay bills." Inside the envelope was two hundred and seventy-five dollars.

That afternoon I lost my fear of the bottom of the barrel. The Lord truly is my provider. Even today, I don't see the businesses that contribute to our income as our provision. They are simply wells God permits us to draw from. If those wells dry up, He will dig another well for us. And He has done that. For it is He and He alone that gives us our provision.

Our part is to understand that the Lord wants what He gives us to flow *through* us. We can never meet our own needs by hoarding. When Rick and I had little, I was careful not to be wasteful, but I found that if I needed milk, I should buy the milk with what I had, trusting God to provide the flow.

Our heavenly Father wants the resources that He gives us to flow through us to others so that we might have the joy of directing some of His abundance to them. He did not design us to be storage tanks, but dispensers, not only of His love, but also of His goodness.

A New Arrangement

One of the fun things about finding old things and bringing them home is displaying them so others can enjoy them and so I can see them every day. Every now and then I get the urge to rearrange, or add a new treasure, or pick up a whole group of treasures and move them to another room. But I always take extremely good care of them, being careful not to set them down until I know that each piece is secure. When I move a teapot, I hold its lid down snuggly as I walk across the floor. When I put a treasure in a new place, to me it's always in a better place than it was before.

I've found that God treats me the same way I treat my treasures when He rearranges my life. He takes very good care of me in the process, and in the end I'm much better off than I was before. A dramatic event in my life proved this to me.

Company was coming. I had already been to the grocery store, and as I scurried around the house making preparations, I gave my four-year-old, Jeremy, a chore to keep

him busy. While I headed outside to store some things in the crawl space under our house, he pulled the linens off his bed for me. But before I could finish what I was doing, I thought I heard him calling for help through the closed windows. I did! He was screaming "Fire!"

I ran into the house and found he had indeed obeyed

me. He had pulled all the linens off of his bed but left them on the floor furnace. I had a fire in the house! But at least the house wasn't on fire. I got Jeremy out and then tried to think of everything I had ever been told about fire. The fire was too big to smother, so I tried pulling the blankets and sheets out the back door. On my third trip, a burning afghan that I grabbed touched the wallpaper, and the fire began to catch here and there. Now the house was on fire!

I ran out the back door and into the next-door neighbors' house and called the fire department. I came back, and there we were—Jeremy and I in the yard, waiting while our house burned. I thought, "We're losing everything. What is everything?" All I could think of were our photos. I looked down at myself and took inventory: Bass Weejuns, jeans, a blue oxford shirt, and a plaid flannel shirt. "This," I thought to myself, "is what I own."

In a very few minutes, I had gone from hostess to homeless. And I had narrowly missed losing a child in a burning house. It was nine days before Christmas.

Thanks to the firemen, our house didn't burn down that day. But it did burn up! As our little family carefully picked through the damp, dark structure our home had become, we realized our lives had just been seriously rearranged.

We spent the next day going through the pile of our burned possessions that the firemen had shoveled onto our front yard, trying to take inventory for the insurance company. The kids waited in the car, the only warm place we had. But if we were pitiful, we didn't know it. After my initial tears, the Lord gave us a remarkable grace to walk through all inconvenience and hard work ahead of us. One friend who came to help remarked, "Whenever I tell someone about your house, I cry. But you're not crying; you're smiling!"

It is true that it is more blessed to give than receive, but sometimes you have to receive, and we had to. Everywhere we turned, our needs were met by loving people. One neighbor washed clothes; another cooked food. Friends brought toiletries; one brought his week's pay; some gave their Christmas vacation time to help. Most important of all, one friend gave us a place to live, complete with furniture, dishes, and linens.

When the offer of this apartment was made to us by our friend who had been divorced for two years, my husband Rick said to me, "When you pray for someone's marriage to be put back together, maybe your house has to burn for it to happen!" He and his wife were both special to us, and we really wanted to see their marriage restored. The Lord did exactly that in the months it took to repair our home. The circumstances of our fire actually did help make it happen. Not only that, we were blessed in other ways, including ending up with a beautiful new house in our fifty-year-old shell.

Before this interruption in our lives, I had thought that making Jesus the Lord of my life meant I would do whatever He asked me to

do. I would just obey. I learned that letting Jesus be the
Lord of my life means that when hard circumstances come
my way, He will take care of me without asking me if my
life can be rearranged. I would never have volunteered for
the experience of that accidental fire so that God could
bless us the way He did. But He worked so much good
from it to us personally, and to other people as well, that
I still thank Him for it. God didn't cause that fire to
happen, but He did allow it. And then He turned a
catastrophe into a blessing. Being a Christian doesn't
just mean "obey." It means "trust" and "obey."

The next time your life is rearranged and in disarray,
remember that He is able to make a great deal of good
ultimately come out of your situation and also to take very
good care of you in the middle of it. Trust Him! He can
do it.

The Most Expensive Flowerpot

My normal MO (modus operandi) for a visit to an antique store is to quickly survey every aisle, looking for an outstanding treasure to take home with me. My eyes scan every booth methodically as I hurry along. On the second time around, I look more leisurely and carefully, but I rarely find anything I missed the first time.

On my second trip through an antique

store one afternoon, I began to give a large, old Victorian sugar bowl that had lost its lid much more attention than it deserved. My disappointment in not finding anything really special in the store must have caused me to make excuses for it—and its price. "Maybe I could put it in a painting." "The design isn't wonderful, but the colors are pretty." And most dangerous of all, "It's the best thing I've found here."

Sixty-five dollars lighter, I took it home with me. After I arrived home, I unwrapped it and put it on the windowsill in my kitchen. Every time I looked at it, I thought, "How could I have done that?" Finally I took a green plant and made it into a very expensive flowerpot so it could at least look useful. But I still wondered how I could have done that.

But that's not the only time I've wondered that! I almost had to pinch myself when a wonderful group of people invited me to participate in a special project. Such an invitation must surely have a heavenly postmark, I thought. How I wanted to do a good job! I asked the Lord to help me be a good servant to this group and to prosper them for their investment in my work. I worked hard to do my best and to be prompt and cooperative. But later, through the faithful wounds of a friend, I became aware that I had been considered somewhat unteachable and even more than a little willful by part of the group. It was a bewildering blow. I thought things had gone well. Had I been living on another planet? To be thought uncooperative or willful filled me with tears of confusion and days of distress. How could I have done that?

The phrase "but Lord..." kept cropping up in my thoughts and prayers, and silently I cried out one night, "But Lord, I wanted to be their servant!" A gentle reply came to my heart, "Don't try to be their servant. Just be My servant."

"Just be My servant." How easy that seems when I purpose to do it, and how impossible it seems when I fail. What does it mean to be His servant? I think it begins with humility. Have you ever decided to look at yourself through someone else's eyes and then seen yourself? I did. And this is what I saw. I saw that while I do want to do everything right, I also want to do it *my* way. This is a crucial issue of the Christian life: replacing the selfish nature we are all born with (that wants to do everything its own way) with His perfect character. Being His servant doesn't mean reforming our selfishness (what the Bible calls self or flesh). It means exchanging *our* way for *His* way.

When I became a Christian, I chose to replace my way with His, but I still have to prefer it moment by moment. I really want to do that so I don't ever have to look back at my whole life and say, "How could I have lived that way?" Have you ever made that exchange—your way for His? It is the very best exchange you could ever make!

Cups of Affection

When most of us think of the Victorian era, what we really like about it is their "stuff." How romantic it is to think about living in a turn-of-the-century home, complete with a turret, lacy gingerbread trim, stained glass, and wraparound porch dripping with cascades of pink roses. Oh, to live such a gracious lifestyle surrounded by such beautiful things!

No doubt about it, the Victorians had some really great things, many of which I would like to own. But the Victorians have shared much more with us than just beautiful homes, furniture, and china. They left the doors of their hearts open for us to see in with the sentiments and verse they hung on their walls, the cards and autographs

they wrote, and the gifts they gave one another.

Cups given as gifts or souvenirs frequently tug at the heart with messages like "Remember me," "Thinking of you," or "To my friend." Their expressions of affection are made even more endearing by their very vulnerability. From that era comes the expression "heart in hand," and much of what they left behind is a picture of a heart offered in an open hand.

One Saturday afternoon as I strolled through a weekend antique market with my father, I spied a dirty little Victorian cup. It wasn't a very pretty cup, but I was captivated by the message on it—"Love the giver." In our day and age, it would take a lot of nerve to give someone a gift like this cup and then ask the recipient to love us for it!

"Love the giver" on the front of that little cup is only half the message. The rest of the message is written in the heart, "Love the giver, for the giver loves you." Why did my heart beat a little faster when I saw that cup? I didn't see exactly what was written on the cup. I saw "Love the Giver"—the Giver. The Bible says in James 1:17 that "every perfect gift is from above, coming down from the Father."

When my eyes see "Love the Giver," my heart hears "The Giver loves you." As I count my gifts and inventory my blessings, I am surrounded by the evidence that my heavenly Father who gives all things loves me! How can I help but love Him? When Psalm 105:1 tells us to be thankful and say so to Him, we are being encouraged to take the time to notice our gifts and our heavenly Father's love for us. If you just look around you and count your blessings, you too will love the Giver, for you will know that the Giver loves you!

Beyond Compare

On a round, skirted table in our parlor an absolutely perfect little teacup and saucer set is perched on top of a small antique photo album. It sits there somewhat proudly because it does not share its little stage with any of the other umpteen teacups I own. The cup and saucer are an elegant ivory color, both rimmed in gold. The genteel simplicity of its design is shown in a single pink rose on the front of the cup and in the center of the saucer, accented by gold leaves. There are no chips or cracks here! I never compare this teacup to any "new" old cups that join my collection. In my opinion, it is also beyond compare as far as anyone else's teacups are concerned.

If you searched really hard far and wide, you might

find a cup just like my flawless little cup. But it still might not be the perfect cup for you. You see, this cup is so special to me because it was chosen for me by my son, Samuel. And I know that he chose it with care and thought that it was just right for me. How wonderful it is when we know something was chosen just for us.

Although the most traumatic experience in my life has been the recent damage to one of my eyes, I have not envied the good vision—even perfect vision—of other artists. I have just been grateful to have been left with good vision in one eye so I could still paint and be an artist. But one day my father

sent me a newspaper clipping about three people—a woman who was an artist, a man, and another woman, all who had retina tears and surgeries similar to mine. As I read their interesting stories, I felt a strong kinship with their experiences until I got to the end. The artist, whose case began with more complications and a more difficult situation than mine, ended up with really good vision in spite of everything. So did the other woman in the story.

My cushion of contentment developed more than a slow leak. I considered the advantage I thought I should have had. After all, many people have prayed for good vision for me for a long, long time. And yet here were two people with results much better than mine—and one of them an artist, no less. I was losing a measure of my gratefulness and beginning to feel short-changed. Even comparing myself to the man in the clipping, who lost his sight, was not a satisfying experience. My disappointment in my own circumstances made it difficult for me to even feel the compassion that he deserved. I was coming to the unsettling conclusion that I hadn't gotten such a good deal after all because I knew somebody else had gotten something better.

In my heart, I began to feather a nest for myself where I could snuggle in with my self-pity and regrets and contemplate the issue of fairness. But one thing kept me from plopping down in it. And that was what God had already taught me about Himself. Would I choose to be disappointed in a God who has said in His Word that He has plans for me, that He will accomplish what concerns me, and that His lovingkindness prevails over me? Or would I choose to trust my heavenly Father and wait—knowing that there is a much bigger picture than what I can see right now? And would I believe that He is working good for me in ways I don't yet see?

When I took my eyes off Him and compared myself to someone else, I began to lose sight of the real beauty of my life and my future. What makes it special is that, just like my little cup, my life was chosen for me—just for me. God has a plan to work everything that happens to me for my good, even when it's something bad. Focusing on that gives me even more confidence in Him and the life plan He has chosen for me. His choice is perfect because He Himself is beyond compare. He not only has a custom-made plan for me, He has a uniquely wonderful plan for you—and only you!

A Priceless Treasure

As I was cleaning my dorm room one day when I was in college, I came across a small Bible with a white leather cover on the bookshelf. It had been a gift to me by an aunt of a young man I had dated for quite some time. In our southern culture, the inference was clear. It was to be carried with a wedding bouquet someday. But that Bible wasn't going to be used in that way because I had ended the relationship. I held the Bible up to my roommate, "What am I going to do with this?" She looked at it and at me and wryly said, "Why don't you read it?"

Another Bible, a very old Bible with a lot of "character," appears in several of my paintings. It has thumb indexes, ragged pages, and a well-used appearance. I appreciate its usefulness to me, but I don't even remember where

I got it. And, as you have probably guessed, I have never read it, either.

The Bible that is dear to me is not the one that is pretty or the one that is old; it is the one I have read and that I still read. It has been a treasure chest to me. When I opened it, I found real life and the very heart of God Himself. In fact, I like to think of the notes I've written and the verses I've underlined as a map to immeasurable treasure. This is treasure that is not hidden at all, but just waiting to be found and possessed. In its pages I have found peace, wisdom, encouragement, hope, instruction, and love.

For that reason, I can recommend your Bible to you as a pretty good place to do some treasure hunting of your own. Even now, it's hard for me to see a Bible without hearing the witty, yet wise, words of my roommate, "Why don't you read it?" A smile crosses my face because I know I have found the right answer to her question—"I have."

The Beautiful Heart

My husband, Rick, says that our house began the way all great endeavors do, as a drawing on a paper napkin. He didn't build it from my sketch on that napkin, but he did build it just from my drawings on graph paper (without blueprints). It took several years of working weekends and holidays to give those drawing three dimensions, but he did it!

When we finally moved in, I stood firmly on a decision I had already made: Nothing was coming into this house unless it was exactly the right thing. Even though this home was several times larger than the home we moved from, I was quite willing to live with wide open spaces and bare walls for months or even years. Experience had taught me well how easy it is to accumulate junk and how hard it is to get rid of!

Well-meaning people offered to fill our spaces with things they didn't want, but I refused as gently and firmly as I could. My goal was not a mansion or a castle, but simply *our* house. Meanwhile, I began my search for things with beauty, meaning, and value. Now after several years, our house has taken on a personality, the personality of the people who call it home.

Just as I am the one who has the "say so" about what comes into my house, I am also the one who has the "say so" about what comes into my heart. Furnishing a heart is a lot like furnishing a home. And people have offered me things I really don't want in my heart, either, that I have had to gently refuse. How can we choose the best treasures? Since I've asked Jesus to live in my heart and make it His home, I only want things in my heart that He is comfortable with. I've learned the value of antiques by acquainting myself with the antiques themselves. In the same way, God's Word tells me all about the Lord. It is there that I can learn what is worthy and like Him and what is not like Him and should be discarded.

I think we all long for a beautiful heart even more than we long for a beautiful home. If you're ready to "redecorate," I recommend the Bible as a "decorator's showcase" of priceless treasures that will never go out of style!

The Missing Treasure

There is one more treasure I wanted to share with you on this visit. I can't show it to you because I don't have it. But I almost had it. In the summer of 1996, the Summer Olympics came to Atlanta which is near to where we live. By the time our family arrived home from a trip to California, the festivities were already underway. So we decided one evening to hop in our van and head downtown. We parked and shopped along the street for available tickets and came up with four for an affordable venue— the Gold Medal baseball game.

There was such excitement in the air and pleasantness among the crowds! We didn't mind walking more than a mile to the stadium through barricaded streets that had become huge sidewalks. As the competition got underway

between Cuba and Japan, we enjoyed absorbing the languages and cultures around us. I wondered how strange the foreigners must think it that Americans like to get up and make the letters YMCA with their arms. I was amused as a voice with a British accent behind us tutored someone in the rules of baseball, explaining that the "fellow would lob the ball."

Suddenly, with a whip of the bat, a foul ball was heading our way! It looked like it might land close by, but there was no way I was going to run and stick an ungloved hand up and risk getting hurt by a baseball. Then it bounced on the aisle steps. Still, there was no way this Southern woman in her favorite summer dress was going to scramble for a souvenir baseball. With one more bounce, it rolled down my aisle to a gentle stop next to my shoe. As I reached down to pick it up, a woman seated near me swooped down and scooped up the ball with glee! All at once, in my mind the ball changed identity. It was no longer a foul ball, it was "my" ball. She took *my* ball! And I felt wronged, even though in "baseball land" such grabs are perfectly legal.

When I examined my heart and the changes in my attitude, I had to honestly admit the truth: I had never really wanted the ball—until she took it! I think it is human nature that sometimes we don't want something until we see that it has value to someone else.

I deeply hope that my sharing some of my treasures with you in our visit together has made you want more treasures of your own. All of these truths that I have found and hold dear can be yours. If it is treasure you want in your heart, go for it (whether you're wearing your favorite summer dress or not)! You won't have to compete for it. The amazing thing is that there is an endless supply of these treasures that are so rare, just waiting for me and for you.